T0243285

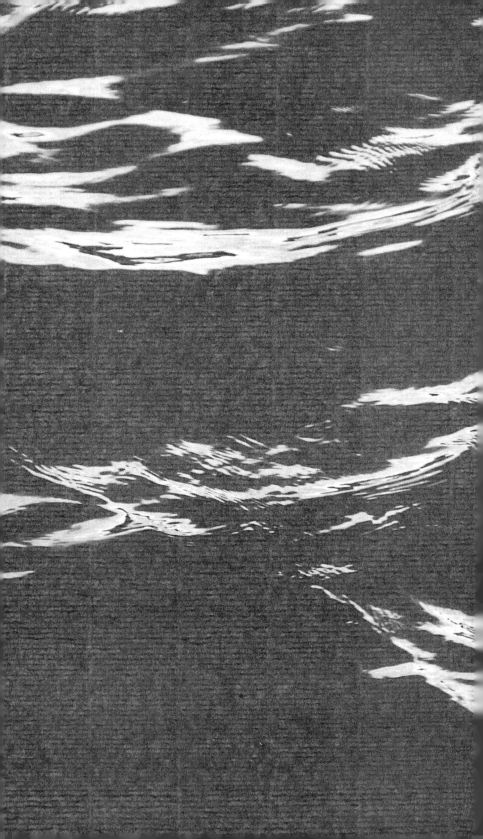

AQUEOUS

Nathanael Jones

pq

Edited by Shane Neilson
Cover and book design by Jeremy Luke Hill
Proofread by Mary Hamilton
Set in Linux Libertine and Acumin Variable Concept
Printed on Coach House Laid
Printed and bound by Arkay Design & Print

LIBRARY AND ARCHIVES CANADA CATALOGUING IN PUBLICATION

Title: Aqueous / Nathanael Jones.
Names: Jones, Nathanael, author.
Identifiers: Canadiana (print) 20240441907 | Canadiana (ebook) 20240441915 |
     ISBN 9780889844759 (softcover) | ISBN 9780889844766 (PDF) |
     ISBN 9780889844773 (EPUB)
Subjects: LCGFT: Prose poems. | LCGFT: Poetry.
Classification: LCC PS8619.O53345 A87 2024 | DDC C811/.6—dc23

The Porcupine's Quill gratefully acknowledges the support of the Canada Council for the Arts, the Ontario Arts Council, and the Ontario Book Publishing Tax Credit.

The Porcupine's Quill respectfully acknowledges the ancestral homelands of the Attawandaron, Anishinaabe, Haudenosaunee, and Métis Peoples, and recognizes that we are situated on Treaty 3 territory, the traditional territory of Mississaugas of the Credit First Nation.

The Porcupine's Quill also recognizes and supports the diverse persons who make up its community, regardless of race, age, culture, ability, ethnicity, nationality, gender identity and expression, sexual orientation, marital status, religious affiliation, and socioeconomic status.

The Porcupine's Quill
130 Dublin Street North
Guelph, Ontario, Canada
N1H 4N4
www.porcupinesquill.ca

Table of Contents

A Botched Science

The Drinking Habits of Masons

In the Absence of a Delta

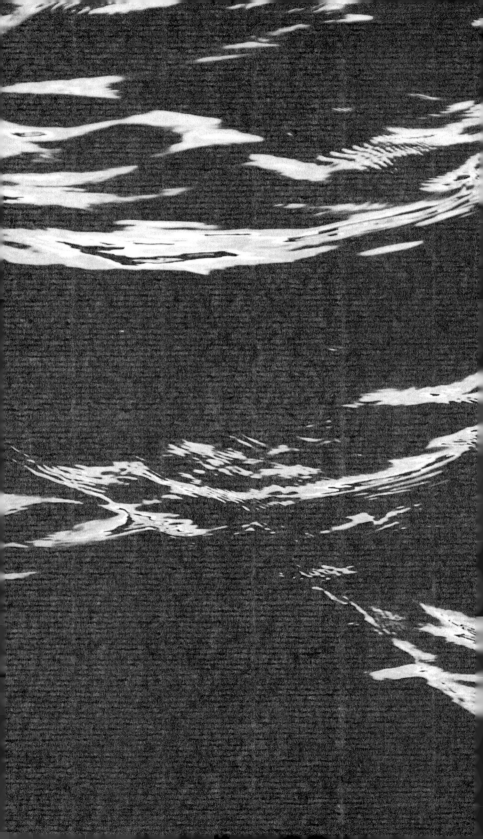

A Botched Science

Installation

A landlocked country, as in, wolverine country; as in, mirroring the motherland's dusky interior; as in, mon pays ce n'est pas un pays, ethnic and cultural hybridity, remembrance, forgetting—not a nation state with a coastline but a cataract, an inability to see beyond the horizon of trauma's incision. A conceptual dilemma.

Note to self: construct a device to simulate the socio-cultural equivalent of an ear stone.

An issue of hearing. Designed to provide an auditory beacon for those adrift in a sea of water droplets, the foghorn stands in for land. A sound artist. Prodding the winding folds of the inner ear, the stones resonate at a frequency capable of tricking the human brain into believing its body is in perpetual motion.

And what if we had never arrived, here.

Bio-mineralization, grains of sand like hair cells, a botched science.

What if the Middle Passage, rather than concluding on the shores of the New World, simply went on forever?

A foghorn in place of a buoy, a buoy in place of a land.

An organic matrix holds together individual particles of silica. The body secretes it: postcolonial mutation. What the body cannot produce itself it can learn to approximate. Papillae searching for a foothold.

Sliding along the ice floes, there are no naturally occurring features of the landscape capable of halting one's momentum.

All life radiates outward from Africa.

Evaporating into the air over the course of a four-hundred-year period, there is no broaching the distance with the naked eye, no clearing the fog of the Atlantic.

A sea of hands pulling a giant parachute over their heads: how an organism of indeterminate size holds its shape. Cybernetic loops. As seen during childhood: a diagram outlining the use of echolocation in certain species of frog-eating bats, their silvery forms skirting the waters.

Outstretched tear ducts hover over the face of unformed ocean. Make do in its absence: a name and time that defy placement. An issue of geography.

A man turns an FM radio into an oscillator before progressing to design tornado sirens, air raid alarms, tocsins. Seated at the workbench, he wrestled with circuitry in an attempt to parse speech from the rush of wind. *My grandparents generation,* he said, albeit they chose Canada over the UK. Lured to the rocks, they heard wind for voices—sirens by another name.

What is a synthesizer if not metal bent and hammered into shapes reminiscent of speech?

A system for translation, and an instrument capable of encoding microtones between the margins of its keys. We found spaces within the official channels. Synthesizers. Tethered to the epicentre of a nonexistent country, shielded in the fog, we listened.

A paradigm expanding upon the concept of double consciousness, out there.

And now, points. Spilling the dregs of the bottle across the table and watching the liquid bead into tight constellations, a thought takes shape. Diaspora.

Tiny voices sounding in the deep—meaning here, on land.

Installation 2

In place of a droning baritone, a carillon, a chirping of steel pans playing a rondeau, an arrhythmia marked by the flight patterns of sea birds: such is the timbre of discontent. It only ever began as a foghorn. The ear finds favour in place of the eye burdened by a rain so fine—so fine it undulates in the wind, a mesh curtain caught between opposing sources of light. Grains of sand for hair cells line the labyrinth of a sounding body, provide the appropriate navigational resonance.

And where are you going in such haste?

All this merely to keep afloat.

Sometimes there is an image, culled out of the air like moisture suffused in the folds of handwoven fibres. A fence named after the phenomenon. Originating in Peru (the Andes more broadly).

We are the divining rods—and all this distance between us: a screen at the service of echolocation, a sieve in the open ocean. Sand at our feet in the landscape and the sand lodged within the recesses of a body.

A constant leaking. Patterns of air: morae, mora.

A sea shell whose self-resonance has been recorded, analyzed for spectral anomalies. Inscriptions gapping a body and its exoskeleton, amplified in post, reveal the muffled screams of jettisoned cargo.

Addendum: we are in fact jetsam, inhabiting ship ledgers.

This territory is not real and yet lifetimes are spent in searching for it.

Coordinates lead to a midden visible only at low tide, the remains of half-eaten crustaceans, ancestral silt: this is wickedness. The readings obtained from these processes are used in the manufacture of the individual bells, correspond to the different sites of conjecture. Some believe the modern migration patterns of pelagic carnivores now reflect the old trade routes.

Carillon: from the Old French, carrion.

The ear stone encases the body, a mollusc shell made primarily of calcium carbonate (in the tropics this is sand). Each a principality fortifying itself, we make the dunes much like a graveyard. What doesn't rise to the surface dredges will uncover, a dying reef, or, how to turn a speaker into a microphone. Invert the process, please. Our bodies like false futures in the sediment. Drawn to land, oceans in our ears.

John, R.

He had to tread water, she said of her father.

Even in shallow seas the limits of vision fail us. Thrown overboard in slack wind or tempest, looking out over the waters: this is how we knew the earth was curved before Magellan, Elcano.

From a seated position, start to kick as if performing the breaststroke.

And as you can see here in the ship logs, the dates are in accordance. The Canary Islands, Cabo Verde—primarily Portuguese and Spanish holdings. Far from any continent, the curve of the earth's surface is caught between a straight line.

Slavers threw the dead and dying overboard.

My father, he fell.

Silica

Inherently tactile, patterns of vibrations enter through orifices adapted to comprehend them as information. Everywhere we are being breached, a siege in name only; it is all the same thing. The Atlantic was transformed into a site of infinite fissures, a crossing of dry river beds; the landscape itself confirms it.

We are all the same thing: the wadi and arroyo, tongues awaiting the rains. Diagonal paths of ingress underlie a form's potency, slope of landscape, erosion.

An organism where hearing predominates, provides the backdrop for a volatile coupling in sand.

Stillborn

The angle at which a child's steps first evaporate beneath them: becoming accustomed to the surrounding weightlessness, a second time. Volatility of place. The shoreline begins here, now there. The water line rises and falls. Memory carries and is carried in the limbs of those learning to walk. What remains are traces of snow and sleet occurring elsewhere, an exodus of rivulets. Inhabiting a geography defined by its lack, we find equivalency in systems of erosion.

Silica 2

Limbs of ashes and oaks line the bottom of an arroyo. How the dead persist amongst the patterns of the living. A country in miniature caught between rocks, trauma minting interstitial ecologies. Boundary fog: where centre and periphery modulate. Here the body politic is indistinguishable from silt, is anomaly, antigen, a strip of beachfront shrinking and swelling. What cannot be both measured and demarcated has no right to land. We are that push and pull of years collapsed in lumens, tide's aggregate. A rolling across the uneven flooring of a shoreface.

A Sound Spoken

An issue of arithmetic: how syntax self-assembles in the mouth. In a foreign tongue, semantic coherence is subject to discordant speeds, varying points of departure.

Please, solve for x.

There is the time of the writing, the passing of virtual time within the writing, and the river mouth.

Selon Derrida, the immaterial are now texts, voices entombed in tomes. A collection of half thoughts abandoned in vocal folds. Phonemes hiccup, part. And if the trumpet should give an uncertain sound, who rouses Leviathan?

Slack Current

Measured from the ice sheets: an ever-changing desert of unprecedented size. Little holds in its featureless waters except oxygen: here the earth is formless, void. Life under siege. If a body should fall or be thrown overboard it can scarcely decompose. Centuries are required to fill a modest pail with sediment. Ours is to wait, to trust to onslaughts of the abacus.

Aerobics

For every air bubble trapped beneath the mud, a fraction of us remains. In the dead spot between currents, no life begins; ever dying, neither can we die. Ferried on the same skin which sustained them, there are no microbes present capable of depleting the abundance of oxygen here. And so, interloping micro-organisms live on in suspended animation. Up and down the sediment column, yet held. More than morgue. Stasis in the great gyre's fulcrum, part of the solution composing clay.

Ferried

In time the promise of the Haitian Revolution hollowed, became husk. We remain someone's cargo. Early Quakers could not yet conceive of the proposed legislation as a lived reality. Develop the means to slake demand; invert the market. We are so free our feet scarcely touch the ground. Twelve years, four months, one week, and four days: landscape considered as time-based, an event.

They aspired to weightlessness, their fingers fashioning abstract shapes in the air.

Held in the earth's orbit through the means of abolitionists, there were no provisions made for the continued existence of those freed (or of slavers). There was no suitable anchor outside of a body. The more, unmoored. We have seen its shores from the bow of a pirogue. Home finds the mother tongue elusive.

We suffer shipwreck. Wanted: a fit of gravity.

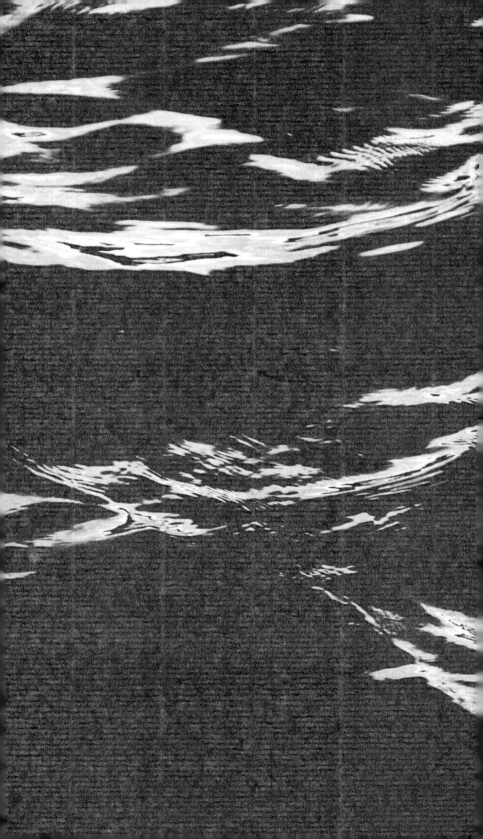

The Drinking Habits of Masons

(park)

In the park I told you to pick up the phone. Go, stand over there. A shallow layer of humus separating our feet from topsoil is now evidence in an argument. See, how the parent rock fractures from so little prodding? The anthropocene as concept. I illustrate through diagrams featuring microplastics in place of seaweed, marine deserts. *Ill-equipped for life on land,* you say, *fetch us a pail and spade.* A fossil I recognize as Ordovician you know as jellyfish. A quarrel high above sea level. *A quarry,* you say, reluctant to make the correction.

(tattoo)

A stick and poke tattoo to match yours, ungainly in how it navigates the dermis. *Remember N, it says, you were late for the gala.* Regions where immune cells congregate, passing a foreign substance across generations: melanism enforced on a deeper, near subcutaneous level. *The reaction does nothing to inhibit the hair follicles,* you say, *their growth, more or less.* Memory takes the form of an overripe peach. A series of points melts into a typeface, the product of conjecture.

(room)

Small perforations in the skin coalesce into a sum yet
to be tabulated. Bodies self-regulate: sweat. When I
tell you we should leave, the words bear the inflection
of the room, the angle at which one leg drapes across
the other. How patterns of air dimple the lips before
one can respond. The web of our relationship renewed
each day.

(laundry room)

A sudden upward coming into view, a tracing of phantom limb limits. Earwig or centipede. An abrasion or rash receives premature diagnosis. Tell yourself it is bed bugs. A disease of the neck. Centipede, definitively.

A sliding doppler. An audible flurry below the occipital.

(sitcom)

A pouring upward in sections, pantomime of excess tension like concrete, catharsis. He said this of a father invoking himself. Post-tensioned slabs are typically flat slabs, band beam ... mostly being kept in compression. A rib cage pretends to fountain then falters, hands as if in worship.

https://www.concretecentre.com/Structural-design/
Building-Elements/Floors/Post-Tension-(PT)-Slabs.
aspx#:~:text=Post%2Dtensioned%20(PT)%20slabs%20
are%20typically%20flat%20slabs%2C,be%20used%20
to%20counteract%20deflections.

(cloud)

The hands of strangers draw my muscles out of atrophy. This is essentially an I-statement; or, how ownership is articulated. In fits and starts. A limbic system misfiring into the dark. The surface of an eye ball drains. Holding up a balled fist and using the side nearest the thumb, in circular motions (counter-clockwise). Dust collects and is expelled. This way. I mean glands.

In place of a river basin: rivulets in shards flooding the plain.

(dark room)

My father hid in dead angles. Said nothing of a hole in the ceiling, how it ate at the present. Please, father, describe that particular shade of black. Draw back remnants of light. When I was a child, your uncle's paintings attempted to finish your sentences. Speak to that. Children splayed on the same back porch where I played. A latent affinity for photography.

(jacuzzi house)

Return to where the fighting started. A deep voice shakes the pillars of a home, revealing weakness. Overtures of foundering; plinth cracks. Small glimpses of how patriarchy conceives arithmetic: one woman with two hair dryers equals four men, no dish rack. Callouses bloom on what remains of the furniture. Like contagion. I whisper to you in the jacuzzi room, below the bed made out of the dining room floor. The power goes out and an unqualified man is hired to fix the problem. Speaker, I think, argue with this man. We are seven to three rooms again after he leaves.

Some of these men have wives.

(sixplex)

A family springs up as a result of other people's trauma. Parquet flooring is upended. A house scissors.

A man buys a shot gun as a matter of course: these are song lyrics, or, a provisional definition for emerging forms of poverty. Meanwhile an assortment of morbid thoughts accumulates at a work site. Small fires catch in puddles during the rain.

The day's shards.

(right hand)

A child's understanding of vital organs. The concept of life expressed as congealed plasma hidden just beneath the skin's surface, as stasis. Finger the puzzle of blood clots and iodine; peace like a river.

(left hand)

A swollen left hand.

A skin hardened against cross-cut lumber, against moisture on cold metal: further expressions of stasis. Soon plagues of callouses seize the entire body.

Join or cause to join together. A section of a poem.

(international tattoo)

A tattoo is also event, an overfamiliarity with sensory array. To be bludgeoned, pour hot tar deep into sinew. Edge ever forward. On the exterior scaffolding work the field negroes: further song lyrics to describe the practice of rubbing palm oil beneath the skin.

(tattoo sequence)

The tattoo arrives not a poem, is already a poem.
These lines are fever, air above mountains.

We needed to leave. Later on the platform, you watched the algorithm gouge grant money from your pocket. *Funds received for works long since completed,* you said, pointing into the distance. With one hand you held a needle over the thumb of the other. We so thoroughly believe in love that stick figures of constellations brand our descendants' retinas.

I say again I want a stick-and-poke tattoo to match yours, begin the disassembly of ball point pens.

Two needles balance in your right hand and mine, our free hands clasped together. *It will be a fairer contest this way*, I tell you.

Two needles, mirrored angles.

It will be a fairer contest.

Unable to point to what is wrong, the shortcut to long term memory proves unnavigable. An email crafted under the care of an ex.

In the gaps between speech acts pregnant with doubt, creativity flourishes. *This is a test*, you say, elongating the last pause. Cruelly endowed, I enlist a vocabulary spanning two languages, several cultures, within and without the continent. Always already partitioned.

(the body, not a body)

Notes on how the future body should work: a fictional character possesses both above average human strength and an inability to grow callouses. Press this hot tea sachet against your thumb. Rubbing it raw, skin fibres congregate like fresh sawdust. *Here*, the lecturer says, pointing enthusiastically into the future, *we make the very foundations upholding corporeality odious*, his words stinging the inner canthus.

In an unhurried voice, a panelist at the same conference confirms that we prime the future for noise music.

(triptych)

All the ways in which a ladder can kill.

A hairline fracture, swollen with rain.

Building a home is akin to launching a boat.

(gallery ephemera)

A red rectangle impersonates a tower block.

Vinyl death.

A flash mob of drones hover over a fallow field.

(exposed wall)

Monday through Friday I take this body apart, invert my relationship to homeostasis. When it is fit for labour bricks give way before it, exposing the drinking habits of masons, the sound of bones breaking throughout the work week. *We tear down to build up,* a voice off camera says, and place much emphasis on this pronoun, we. Sheets of insulation like a mural, colour in fields. Through demolition we prove the maxim about acts of creation. Pick up spray cans, fan out across the city.

(bed)

We call it a steal.

A dome in place of fog.

When I did sleep I dreamt about jacuzzi house.

(scaffolding)

A knot in place of a joint. An itch in damp weather.

Of me the crew says, *He's the poet; he's learning about physical labour.* The Super says, *You need a practical epistemology of the body,* handing me a framing square. *Aaaa body,* I whisper.

Here, walk this plank blindfolded. Before I can protest, he removes charred pine wood from his outer canthus, batting his lashes clean.

We aren't standing on anything.

(Doe, J.)

A sex toy is given a name, a birth date and place of origin. These are subsequently lost by the owner. Hi [blank], how are you? a sparsely furnished apartment or flat where small talk fades, two adults disrobe. *No; please, hold me here.* Beyond the door's threshold. Now, imagine these two adults are black or indigenous, rarely talk to one another except to pass notes on the weather. Place them in a city whose emotional temperature is equivalent to that of Berlin. Pour the necessary concrete, cast adequate shadows.

(commercial break)

A young black man's homelessness helps sell toothpaste.

An interracial fist bump lasts two tenths of a second: how tenuous our narratives of progress are, how predicated upon the human desire to edit. Reality another naturally occurring material springing up out of the ground. Supple.

(foundations)

A temperament of dirt found beneath homes. Akin to clay. Submerged, a different kind of house negro works the basement. Shoveling soot cakes the skin anew, piebald and temporary. A walking hyperbole, I blast concrete definitions into dust, meander the deepest channels of the earth. Today's home is slated to become a coliseum.

(roof)

A disgruntled chorus of carpenters shout, *Grace to the parapet.* Yes, give it adequate grace.

A roof with a porous membrane; or, a theatre of ideals we build together, leaking upwards.

Looking down from a great height with the urge to jump, our beam shudders.

(nest)

A loosely knit group of aged pack rats attend to the work site: concertinaed piles, butts. Stud walls divest their hoardings, nascent forms of agency. *I-beams are not playthings,* one says, before holding up a broken metacarpal. Build a home of cardboard first, then begin with the wood. These words I collect in the makeshift bathroom stall, inadvertent mimicry.

(stilt house)

An estuary where I-statements become lost and fester: take responsibility in the mire. Construct active sentences. Find work through the creation of previously nonexistent problems as a travelling salesperson. Move this table saw, then, prepare a party for the plumbers.

Always already below sea level.

(fibre optics)

The body as commodity. A thing used to haggle over projected use cases. Body as algorithmic fluctuation. Numbers in other people's mouths. Make it excluded from this category (people): body not people. Gravedigger, one of two clowns. Body submerged within itself, buried below birch plank. Brown body similarly unhoused, entrenched beneath layers of concrete and linoleum. A stain like fog in a pine beam.

Shoveling underwater.

Expectation: the right tool makes butter of fresh lumber. How work is devalued. Twins saw in unison, the blade severing sinew. What eyes do to labour.

(sous-sol)

The diminutive, dark-skinned-poet-that-could, or, masculinity in making.

Dear labourer, mix cement without dust as a byproduct.

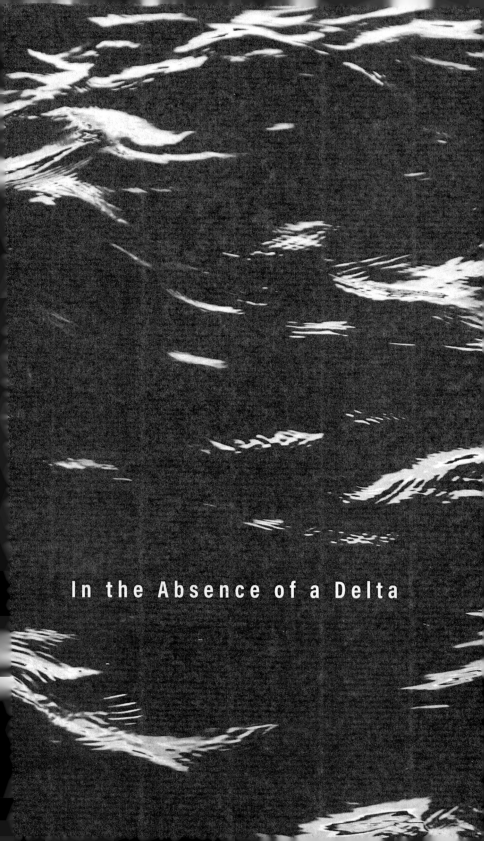

In the Absence of a Delta

A skiff above shallow seas, peopled archipelagos.

White dust applied becomes second skin. Butoh.
Négritude.

A latent autonomy leaches into the water of the Saint Lawrence: valley air. In the absence of a delta, we are that all too crucial sediment lacking on the tongue. In our indigence we would people the mouths of pure laine speakers.

Blacken the lips a second time. Lacking a body, and so, absent from the conversation.

(Well acquainted with this term, lack.)

Essentially, there are and have never been any blacks here to be niggers.

Individual quarry stones, chipped and bruised into silence. Identity a much-hated performance. We work and dig. Then lyrics come.

An incision made at the bridge of the retina.

Lips parted, seize without seeing, scalp-pulled. Here, blackness is absence: we populate impossible spaces, islands like shoals. Lacking the necessary tectonics to form sand natively, coral from the Caribbean is shipped north. Sloughs rapids. Slurs speech. It is the concept of a delta, embodied.

High resolution images of grass blades.

A nascent predilection for AstroTurf®.

The community is not here, does not come by observation.

A scattershot comprehension of geography: not, this here is all black people, but rather, this is where blacks may be found. Several inarticulate voice actors narrating over an empty, nine block radius, vacant streets. A theme park without rides.

A landscape comprised of seemingly disconnected performances. Coalescing, or, the ways in which language resists fragmentation.

In colour, burgundy.

Too literally ocean. We a note cluster played in desperation and plotted across eight axe-ease. Syntax described as halting; we are halting.

Inconsolable, and yet insisting on consolation.

(interlude)

How to operate and clean wounds:

A series of open-ended grievances squeezed between framing studs, our relationship is constantly prompting reenactments of history (Yves Klein's *Leap* ...).

A home where windows multiply—life becomes a reverse bellows.

Boulevards and cul-de-sacs recede into the horizon behind us. Duplexes mutate, assume cumulative shapes.

How a city incubates its own strains of wonder, or, propagates itself. Children as playgrounds.

To adult is to enact the impossibility of a return, indefinitely. So is it with us.

(interlude for Marie-Joseph Angélique)

Days accumulate on the backs of the subaltern.

Metal for clay: a group of notes collecting around a harmonic inversion.

In the silence of the Papal Briefs we tiptoe around the city. Holding candlesticks of Benin bronze, vigil fires are lit for Angélique. A call to remembrance. Distracted graffiti.

This is the day following April tenth.

Domestics and sawyers, arsonists. Holiday.

(a further interlude)

The skin assumes a fractured quality: a topography haunted by the whip and lance, palm oil. Perpetual haptic resonance.

Physical descriptions in print and on the web belie the slow progress of language through canals, rift valleys, wadis. In this way all grope at noonday as if in darkness. A finger in a lash wound: how to touch across centuries.

Dust in the algorithm. Humanity is no longer an aspirational quality for humanity. To emote in earnest: blink twice if you are struggling through successive waves of captchas. When a motorcycle is not a crosswalk. Click here to confirm it.

(a further interlude, continued)

Sapphire; Sambo; Mulatto Wench; Angry Black Man; Head Nigga in Charge; Song and Dance Man; Train Porter; Dread; Mammy, Pickney; Mrs. Butterworth; Jezebel; Buck Niggers; Jigaboos; Spooks—a lingering presence, a seemingly overdeveloped humanism, on the one hand, usurped by and for those expressly permitted into this category, and on the other, live rounds, shells, buckshot (open season).

Identity is a rhizome of conflicts.

A wavetable lookup.

Computer opera.

A borderline personality occupying the theoretical space between different women, mothers, aunts, sisters. The sum of their accruing masses, or, a time that is decidedly not a physical object. The lifespan in progress, an ongoing experiment with gender. Another version of this hypothesis results in a professional athlete; not poetry, conceptual art.

A father as punitive measures.

A mother and a woman and would-be women caught between two mirrors.

Sons in orbit.

(this is that same interlude)

Too literally ocean, emptied: a swarm of bees in place of a Yoruba deity; a low cloud of gulls over water; not the individual instance but the wood block's precognition of the millions of splinters it engenders— identity in and through dissolution. Diaspora.

(a final interlude[1])

1. Montreal as a collection of stacked terraces groping the sheer slope of a wedge. Vistas cross streets, puncture tower blocks in the cold. We stand in windows, carparks, ball courts, dot the concrete. Above and below. Building causeways across lines of sight, espying each other.

Acknowledgements

An excerpt of "Installation" first appeared in *Timber* Issue 14.1 of *TIMBER Journal.*

Thank you to Hayley for all your support during the making of this collection. Thank you to my family: Greta, Terence-Josef, Noel, Nikkia, and Neishel.

Thank you to the fellow passenger on the Barrington bus who I know only as Mark. I am still writing poetry: thank you God.

I acknowledge the support of the Canada Council for the Arts.

About the Author

Nathanael Jones was born in Montreal, Canada, and studied art and literature at NSCAD University (BFA 2014) in Halifax, Canada, and at the School of the Art Institute of Chicago (MFA 2017) in Chicago, United States. He is the author of two chapbooks: *ATG* (HAIR CLUB, 2016) and *La Poésie Caraïbe* (Damask Press, 2018). He has exhibited and performed at galleries, performance venues, and alternative spaces in Canada, the United States, and the U.K., and his work has been published online and in print with *Aurochs, DREGINALD, Infinity's Kitchen, Parallax, Ghost Proposal, Present Tense Pamphlets, Funny Looking Dog Quarterly, Partial Press, Heavy Feather Review,* and *TIMBER Journal*. He is a recent recipient of a Canada Council for the Arts grant.

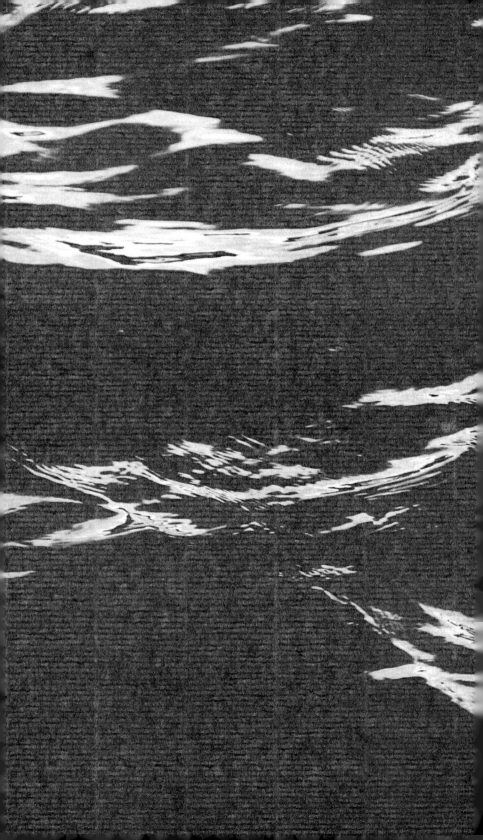